The Five Senses

Seeing

Rebecca Rissman

Heinemann Library
Chicago, Illinois

www.heinemannraintree.com
Visit our website to find out more information about Heinemann-Raintree books.

To order:

☎ Phone 888-454-2279

🖳 Visit www.heinemannraintree.com to browse our catalog and order online.

Edited by Rebecca Rissman and Catherine Veitch
Designed by Ryan Frieson and Kimberly R. Miracle
Original illustrations © Capstone Global Library
Illustrated by Tony Wilson (pp. 10, 22, 23)
Picture research by Tracy Cummins
Originated by Heinemann Library
Printed in China by South China Printing Company Ltd

14 13 12 11 10
10 9 8 7 6 5 4 3 2 1

Library of Congress Cataloging-in-Publication Data
Seeing / Rebecca Rissman.
p. cm. -- (The five senses)
ISBN 978-1-4329-3679-2 (hc) -- ISBN 978-1-4329-3685-3 (pb)
QP475.7.R57 2010
612.8'4--dc22
2009021784

Acknowledgments

The author and publishers are grateful to the following for permission to reproduce copyright material: Age Fotostock pp. **17** (© Mirek Weichsel), **23 D** (© Mirek Weichsel); Corbis p. **19** (© karan kapoor/Cultura); Getty Images pp. **9** (Jonathan Kirn), **11** (Bob Elsdale), **20** (Michael Denora), **21** (altrendo images); Photolibrary pp. **4** (Polka Dot Images), **5** (LWA/Dann Tardif), **13** (Imagesource Imagesource), **16** (Aurelie and Morgan Da); Shutterstock pp. **6** (© Katarzyna Mazurowska), **7** (© Monkey Business Images), **8** (© Kristian Sekulic), **12** (© Losevsky Pavel), **14** (© Jacek Chabraszewski), **15** (© Ben Heys), **18** (© David Lade), **23 A** (© Kristian Sekulic), **23 C** (© David Lade).

Cover photograph of a girl making a frame with her fingers reproduced with permission of Photolibrary (Fancy). Back cover photograph of a close-up of a woman's eyes reproduced with permission of Shutterstock (© Kristian Sekulic).

The publishers would like to thank Nancy Harris, Yael Biederman, and Matt Siegel for their assistance in the preparation of this book.

Every effort has been made to contact copyright holders of any material reproduced in this book. Any omissions will be rectified in subsequent printings if notice is given to the publisher.

Contents

Senses

We all have five senses.

We use our senses every day.

Seeing and touching are senses.

Tasting, smelling, and hearing are also senses.

How Do You See?

eye

You use your eyes to see.

Your eyes are in your head.

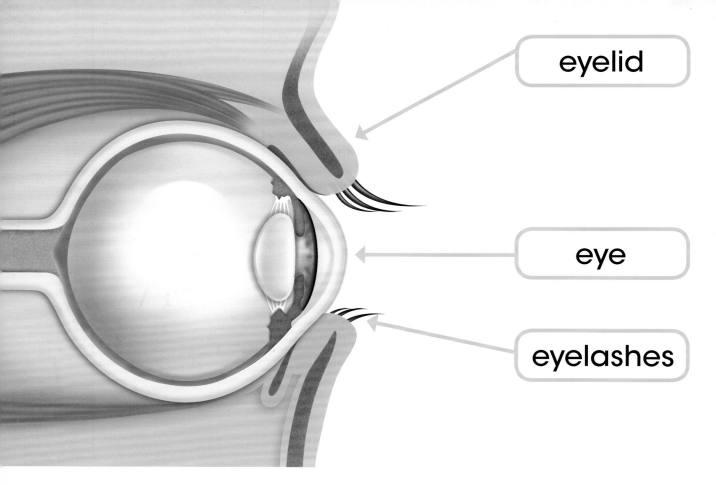

eyelid

eye

eyelashes

Your eyes are round like balls.
Your eyes have many parts.

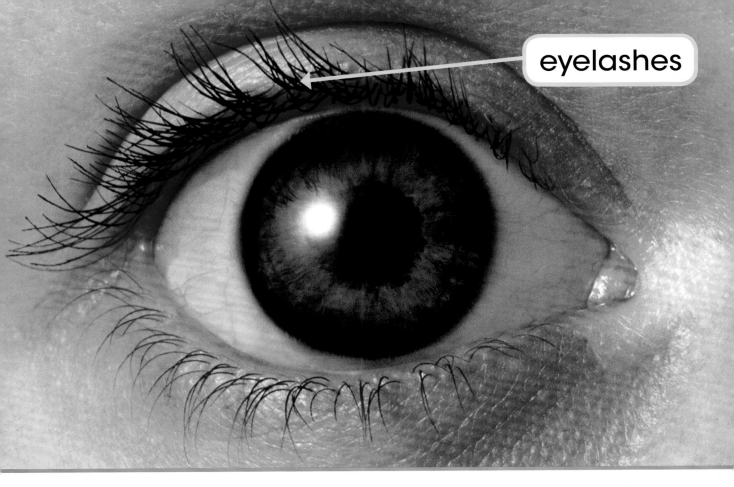

eyelashes

Your eyelashes help keep dirt out of your eyes.

What Can You See?

Your eyes can see color.

Your eyes can see shapes.

Your eyes can see things that are near.

Your eyes can see things that are far away.

Your eyes can see big things.

Your eyes can see small things.

Protecting Your Eyes

Sunglasses can protect your eyes.

eyelid

Your eyelids can protect your eyes.

Helping People See

glasses

Some people wear glasses to help them see.

Some people do not see at all.
They use other senses to help them.

Naming the Parts of the Eye

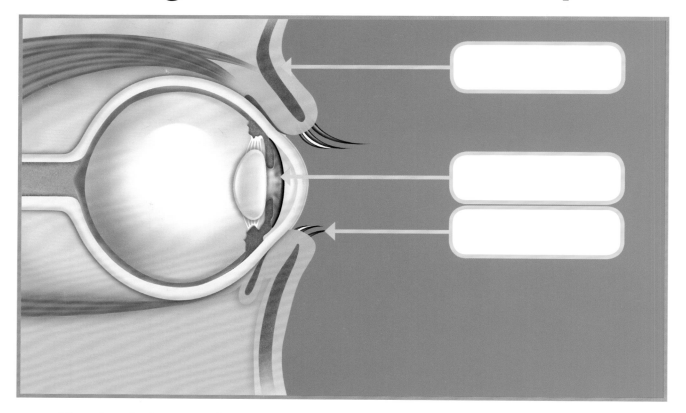

Point to where these labels should go.

eyelid   eye   eyelashes

Answer on page 10.

Picture Glossary

eyelashes small hairs on your eyelid that help keep dirt out of your eye

eyelid part you can use to cover and protect your eye

protect keep something or someone safe

sense something that helps you smell, see, touch, taste, and hear things around you

Index

Note to Parents and Teachers

Before reading

Explain to children that people use five senses to understand the world: seeing, hearing, tasting, touching, and smelling. Tell children that there are different body parts associated with each sense. Then ask children which body parts they think they use to see. Tell children that they use their eyes to see.

After reading

• Show children the diagram of the eye on page 22. Ask them to point to where the labels "eyelid," "eyelashes," and "eye" should go.

• Explain to children that some people are visually impaired. These people may wear glasses to help them see. Others may use a cane to get around. Some visually impaired people read Braille. Find an example of Braille text and encourage children to feel the bumps.